THIS BOOK BELONGS TO:

____

Made in the USA
Monee, IL
10 September 2021

77779501R00069